ISBN: 9798731350532

Reining in Educator Stress
A guide to help educators reduce stress and stay in the
game.

By Michael Rountree

This book is dedicated to my past, present, and future
students. You are the "Why" in what I do.

Purpose of this book:

At some point in their career, most educators experience great amounts of frustration and stress which can lead to burnout. The number of educators that leave the field within the first five years is staggering. I've researched many articles that report as much as 50%. This number is very concerning to me, and really should be to the rest of the country. I'll talk about many of the reasons, but most importantly, I want this book to focus on what can be done to help lower this alarming statistic.

Every profession or industry has federal, state, and local policy that they have to follow. Education is no different. I would highly encourage every educator to follow and meet these requirements. If you feel like policy should change, be constructive, professional, follow the correct protocol, and uphold the integrity of our profession.

The information in this book comes from my personal experiences as an educator since 1995, and from very experienced educators that I personally respect and admire.

I want to be very clear on the purpose or intent of this book. It is simply to give educators ideas that will give encouragement and help them to want to stay in the game. It is NOT a gripe session. It is NOT intended to diminish, point out shortcomings, or single out any individual or group of people. I hope every reader will find encouragement, hope, and ideas that will strengthen their "Why" in this amazing and rewarding profession.

In the Spring of 2019, I was nominated by the administrators at Spearman, Texas I.S.D. for the Texas Rural Education Association Teacher of the Year award. I filled out a lengthy application that took a couple of weeks, submitted it, and won! It was one of the biggest honors of my life. My family, friends, and fellow educators were so supportive and congratulatory. It was something that I needed very badly, that I'll talk about more at the end of this book.

I attended the TREA conference in Fort Worth, Texas that summer and gave the key-note speech in front of rural educators from all over the state. I went to various breakout sessions for the first couple of days and heard expert speakers on topics that affect rural educators and learned so much. But, the thing that stood out most was the genuine, sincere, concerns and feelings they had for kids. Everything that was mentioned was about the kids in rural schools.

On my way home, I told my wife, Jennifer, that I had found my "Why" again after many years, and I felt the strong need to give back in some way. After serving many years in education, teaching many different subjects and grade levels in five different school districts, I felt rejuvenated, excited, and loved being an educator more than ever. Not only do I want this energy to continue, but I feel the strong calling to help other educators sift through their frustrations and focus on why we do what we do in schools. The information in this book is not an exhaustive list, but one that will help just about anyone in any profession, especially those serving in education.

Chapter 1
Runaway Horse
(Negativity can be a Cancer)

I only had four and a half more years, and I would be eligible for retirement. It had been a great twenty-three years. I worked with so many amazing young people, made so many friends, and loved the subjects I taught. My current district, Spearman, Texas I.S.D. paid me well, as far as teacher pay goes. Life was good at home. It seemed that the kid's lives had settled, my marriage was great, and we were living in the country, enjoying our animals, so things should be great, right? I liked my principal and superintendent and got along well with everyone I worked with. I had come to the point in my career, where I knew my content better than ever, and my students did very well on the state standardized test. So, why did I constantly think about retirement?

It had become a survival game. I worried about the constant changes and requirements from the state and local district and wondered if my limitations could survive another four and a half more years. I put so much focus on the state test, and it was causing me to be miserable.

I would wait in anticipation during the summer for the call from my school administrator saying the scores came in, and I should come in and take a look. The great scores came with a "Nice Job" or "Congratulations," which was very nice.

School would start for the next year, and it would begin with the importance of doing even better on this year's test, implementing a new program, or implementing new modifications on those with special needs. I would see worry and fret on the faces of the new teachers and scowls and arms folding on the veterans. These ruts of frustration were beginning, even before the first day of the school year. I absolutely hated the first and second week of the school year. I just wanted the kids to come, so I could shut my classroom door and teach the subjects that I love to teach.

I would sit in these meetings until I couldn't stand it anymore, so I would go to the teachers' lounge to refill my coffee where I would overhear a group of teachers complaining. "How in the world do they expect us to fit the new state standards into the nine million others?" "Are they going to provide extra help with the special needs kids?" "Do they expect us to do brain surgery on some of these kids?" "I have all the bad kids in one class! It's going to be the class from hell!" "I hope this new principal is a strong disciplinarian!" "Those teachers have no idea what I do in the office!" "I hope the principal makes that family take a bath. They stink up the whole school!" I bet you could probably add many more to this list if you thought about it for just a minute. I wonder if Mrs. Beadle from Little House on the Prairie had some of the same gripes? I bet she definitely wanted to take a paddle to Willie more than she already did.

The constant challenges in education can cause us to have a default setting of negativity and griping when the frustrations occur. It usually happens in a step by step pattern…

1. Challenges occur.
2. Fear and worry set in the brain.
3. A fiery storm of words come out of the mouth, and someone is blamed and verbally ripped to shreds.
4. The one challenge has just festered into two or three.
5. We eat chocolate and gain weight!
6. The process starts over and nothing is resolved

Does this sound about right?

I've heard many times over in the "venting sessions, "I know I shouldn't gripe, but I just need to get it out." I used to believe that, but I'm not sure if it doesn't do more harm than good. It can become a cancer of worry, fear, and fretting that can fester and have a devastating effect on some people.

One year I worked with an elementary teacher that was going through a nasty divorce and naturally, she would come to school and vent to her fellow teachers. By the end of the year, two of those teachers that lent an ear to her issues ended up getting a divorce as well. I don't know the details of their situations, but I've always wondered if the first teacher had unknowingly planted some really bad seeds. This negativity can become a cancer that is much like a runaway horse, one that becomes out of control, gains momentum, and usually leads to disaster.

Before we go on a venting session, take a minute or two to collect your thoughts before you say a word. Be aware of what's going on around you, investigate, discover, and collect information. Take a minute to think about the big picture. Administrators, teachers, and coaches may work in the same building, but our worlds are usually very different.

It's very true that being an educator comes along with so many frustrations, but before we get off of this runaway horse, I want to ask you to do one more thing. Take out a sheet of notebook paper, list as many complaints and frustrations that you can think of and share them with a fellow educator. Share them and get passionate about it. Explain the problems in detail and shake your finger and say a few choice words and talk about how stupid something or someone is. You may use words such as looser, stinky, arrogant, and know it all!

Then tear it into small pieces and repeat after me...I (state your name) know these kinds of challenges come with being an educator. I also know that if I dwell on them, they can cause great stress affecting my health, my family, my friends, and my students. I also acknowledge that I cannot do much or anything about some of them, but I can lower my stress level and have a positive impact on those around me, if I change my way of thinking and start doing some things differently. So, let's talk about those changes because if we are unhappy, stressed, and frustrated, the rut of negativity will grow deeper and worse, it will spread to others including your students. Make a decision to get off this runaway horse now!

Teacher Funny...I love it when my students come back from being absent and ask if we did anything in class. I always respond with, "Yes, we had a party with cake and punch!"

God, grant me the serenity to accept the things I cannot change, courage to change the things I can, and wisdom to know the difference...

Chapter 2
Joining Up
(Be Flexible)

My fourth year, I taught 5th grade Social Studies and Science at Anne Whitney Elementary in Hamilton, Texas. I had just started to become pretty comfortable with the content. I enjoyed the subjects that I taught and thought I was just becoming a pretty decent teacher when my principal called me into his office and said, "Mr. Rountree, I want you to teach 5th grade Reading and Writing next year." I wasn't sure what to say. I strongly felt I was meant to be a Social Studies teacher because I loved history so much, and I had lots of fun doing the simple experiments with the kids in Science, and now I had to change?

I really liked my principal, Randy Edwards, and agreed with much hesitation. I passed my friend and long-time teacher, Dan Raibourn, in the hall on my way back to class. He saw the confusion on my face and asked, "What's up?" I looked at him in astonishment and said, "I have to teach Reading and Writing next year." He just laughed and shook his head and said a few words that I'll always remember, "You have to roll with the flow in small schools, and be flexible. It comes with the territory. " I laugh at myself every time I think about how bent out of shape I had become over the change, and Dan was exactly right.

The next year our school adopted the Reading Renaissance Program, and I was in charge of implementing it for four 5th grade classes. We established reading levels and point goals. We adjusted the schedule to give the students 80 minutes of reading time in class every day, and away we went. I tried to check reading logs and sit with struggling readers every week, and as we read together, I got to know my kids.

We would go to the library together, where I would help get the perfect book for them. We looked at fiction, non-fiction, the number of typed pages and illustrations, and the size of the print. We would read a chapter, then I would ask questions to check for comprehension.

My heart really went out to those kids that were struggling readers, so I started looking into why they were struggling. I learned so much about dyslexia, phonological issues, and learning disabled kids.

Most of my kids were rural country kids that enjoyed playing with their dogs and cats, riding their horses, fishing, and hunting. I found *Ole Yeller, Where the Red Fern Grows, the Hank the Cowdog* series, and I used these books to start the love of reading and then I could branch out from there.

One day I was talking to one of my 5th graders about his horse and I told him that I have horses and that my dad was a farrier and a trainer. I told him stories about me and many of my horses and how I used to get home from school and ride them until after dark. This little guy looked at me and said, "Mr. Rountree, why don't you write a book?"

My first juvenile chapter book in the series is *Gunpowder, Tales of a Wise-Cracking Cowpony*. The second is *Gunpowder the Cowpony Goes to Cowboy School*, and the third is *Gunpowder, Rivals on the Ranch*. They are perfect for rural kids that need a chapter book to get them started and all horse enthusiasts. By the way, I didn't write all three that year, but if my principal hadn't made me change, I highly doubt there would be a Gunpowder series.

My one and only year as a principal was at the big town of Cranfills Gap, Texas. We had 122 students in Pre-K through 12th grade. This little school is rich in Norwegian and German history and culture. It is settled in a beautiful valley surrounded by hills that were covered in cedar and broad leaf trees. It even had a clear creek running through the middle of town. My first day of being a principal, I thought I would be there forever. I could look out my office window and see nothing but cattle grazing in the valley and those beautiful hills.

We had a few weeks before the students would show up, so my superintendent and friend Vince Gilbert, the maintenance man and friend Mr. Abraham, and I started stripping the old wax off the floor of the cafetorium and bathrooms. We put chemicals down and started buffing over and over and over. I'm pretty sure that floor had six or eight coats of wax that had built up.

Since we were so small, I also had the job of teaching 4th and 5th grade math in the morning for a couple of hours, to which I gladly agreed since I had 4th and 5th grade teaching experience. I think I taught four 4th graders, which was the entire 4th grade class and six or eight 5th graders, again the entire class.

Sometime before the first semester was over, one of our bus drivers was not able to drive anymore, so guess who became the bus driver in the morning and afternoon for several months. Yep, it was the principal/elementary math teacher/part time maintenance guy. It was yours truly.

I don't think I mentioned that we could only afford a part time counselor a couple of days a week, so I filled those shoes when needed. I attended every in town basketball and football games and most out of town games. Several times, I had to drive the team when the coach hurt his back. Being flexible at Cranfills Gap was an understatement, and I decided being a classroom teacher was much simpler and suited me better, but I will never forget my one and only year as a principal. I learned so much about that part of being an educator. I learned a lot about people including myself and enjoyed the new knowledge that challenged me to be where I am today and I want to thank Vince Gilbert and the good folks of Cranfills Gap for giving me that opportunity.

Since 1995, I have taught elementary resource special education, 4th grade-all subjects, 5th grade all subjects, junior high resource special education, 6th grade World Studies, 7th grade Texas History, 8th grade American History, 6th and 7th grade Math, 8th grade English, 9th grade World Geography, 10th grade regular and AP World History, 11th grade regular and AP and dual -credit American History, 12th grade regular and dual-credit American Government and Economics, principal of a Pre-K through 12th grade school, and drove a school bus at five different rural schools. Whew! I bet Dan is really laughing right now.

Many years ago, I had the privilege of meeting and eating lunch with World Champion Team Roper Walt Woodward at one of his team roping schools in Baton Rouge, Louisiana. My friend and team roping partner, Sonny Miller worked with Walt and knew him very well.

Walt traveled all over the United States conducting team roping schools and had the request for good, well trained roping horses, but he was too busy with the schools to sell horses, so he told us that if we found good horses, videoed them in action, and mailed the videos to him, he would make sure we were well compensated. Sonny and I were always looking for an extra dollar, so we went on the hunt.

Usually, Sonny would do the videoing while I roped off the horse being shown, especially if it was a heading horse and then vice-versa. I would miss time after time because I wasn't familiar with the horse, and the horse didn't know me, and I was trying to make the horse conform to me. This wasn't working well at all, and then it dawned on me that I would have to conform to the horse, and I started catching. I had to be flexible in not only my actions, but more importantly in my attitude and mind. I try to have the same mindset with my students, what I teach, and the administrator's requirements.

A very important trait in being a great teacher/horse trainer is being able to communicate and join up with your student/horse. If I want my horses and students to succeed, I have to first be flexible to them as an individual and want a relationship. How often should this be done? Every day if necessary.

I have about a gazillion spirit t-shirts that I've collected over the years. These are the kind that we are allowed to wear at school on game day, and most of them have an aspiring message on the front or back, and more often than not, the word "coachable" is thrown in there. I'm not a sports coach and definitely not an expert on any sport, but I would definitely agree that athletes must be coachable. They have to be disciplined and trained to become the best they can be. They have to work as a team, every person doing their part and being able to be flexible on the court or field. Would you agree that maybe all educators should be "coachable?" I think so, even the old cronies like myself.

Don't you just love it when some workshop guru or curriculum expert tells you what you are doing wrong, and if you implement this new program, scores will go up and all the world's problems will go away? Maybe that's not what they are saying, but I can tell you, that's what a lot of educators are hearing. I have been to enough workshops and implemented more than enough programs to choke a horse. Side note… I really don't want to choke a horse. Not sure where that saying came from… but you get my drift.

One thing has remained constant in all this change. I, the educator, get to deliver the new program, etc. I generally don't have much control over the What and When, but I have a lot of input in the How and Why, and That is where the impact is made.

I have a sign in my classroom that reads:

We Learn.
We must be tested, and then we find a failure place
and find out where we are broken.
We adapt...change...This is the tough part!
Then we adopt the change, and it becomes a part of
who we are.

This sign is just as much for me as it is for my
students.

Educator Funny….Speaking of Concession Stands,
have you ever really thought much about the so-called
food that is served in them? We open gallon cans of
oil that looks like cheese and gallon cans of dark stuff
that looks like chili, we heat them up, pour them over
chips, and sprinkle a few jalapenos over the top and
yum, right? If I am lucky, I get to sneak away and
watch the band and football players for a few
minutes. I always notice some young loving couple,
smiling and laughing, cuddled up in a blanket, sharing
this gourmet dish of nachos and probably having the
night of their life??

Here's a concession stand tip...Take a can of Sprite
and empty it in the cheese when heating it up. Gives it
a little more flavor and loosens the stuff up a bit.

Chapter 3
Touch of a Fly
(Positive Energy)

When the 2018-19 school year started, I was miserable. I drive a bus route for extra money, which I don't mind at all. I'm a morning person, so I get to watch the sun come up, drink a cup of coffee, while listening to an audible or podcast before I pick up my first rider. After a 50-minute route, I would step off the bus and into the school and begin the long walk to my classroom. Again, I would ask myself if I would make another four and a half years until retirement. This was not good and I knew it had a very negative impact on my students. I desperately wanted to change, but I had no idea how.

The first week back our principal and my good friend, Kelly Carrell, called us into the library for a staff meeting. He was excited, and wanted to share something that he experienced that summer. He attended a conference where Jon Gordan, author of *The Energy Bus*, was the keynote speaker. He was so moved by the speaker that he bought *The Energy Bus* and its sequel, *The Positive Dog* for all of the teachers to read.

Now, over the years, I've had a few principals assign books for us to read, and honestly, I wasn't excited about any of them until now. When Mr. Carrell started to describe the book, I heard several words over and over, and they were "Positive" and "Energy." I had read several "Self Help" books before and have never been much of a fan, but this time, things were different, maybe because I knew I needed something fresh and new and it related directly to teachers.

I actually had bought the book on audible and listened to it on my bus route before his order arrived. As a matter of fact, I listened to it twice. I would meet Mr. Carrell in the hallway in the morning and share exciting things that I had thought of as a result of the book. He got excited because I was excited, so he asked me to share a little about the book at our next staff meeting, and I gladly accepted.

I needed a win, bad! I needed something to get me out of this funk. I asked Mr. Carrell for a Positive Energy Bus Ticket, posted Jon Gordan's rules in my class and read the next book, *The Positive Dog*. I made signs of Jon Gordan's quotes to post around my classroom and added a few more of my own.

They include:
- ✓ Feel Blessed, not stressed (count your blessings)
- ✓ Choose Faith, not Fear (Fear causes stress that is difficult to control)
- ✓ Blaming others keeps us from getting better (we have to own our mistakes before improving)
- ✓ Be a friend, help others
- ✓ Rest your mind, turn off your device
- ✓ Sleep, Eat Healthy, and Exercise
- ✓ It's Nice to be important, but it's more important to be Nice
- ✓ Look Sharp, Feel Sharp, and Be Sharp
- ✓ Show Love, Care, Forgiveness, and Trust
- ✓ Have Fun and Laugh Often (my favorite)
- ✓ Turn Challenges into Opportunities

I started to feel a difference in my attitude and consequently my students liked me better which meant I got more from them and everyone benefited. I would recommend the books to any educator, but know for things to change, you have to change and that takes much more than a cheer and a show.

I personally and totally believe that educators are ordinary people that do extraordinary things, just like so many of our historical heroes. We are imperfect people who want to always get better.

If you're struggling with positivity, write down five things for which you are most thankful for. Don't just list general things like….God, Family, Health, etc., but go deeper. I'm thankful for God's amazing love that he has for me and so thankful for his grace. I love my wife and each and every one of my kids. You get the picture.

Think about the greatest accomplishment in your teaching career to set the mood of positivity. How many lives have you impacted in a positive way? Do you remember a particular student that really tugged at your heart?

The rut of griping and negativity was deep and it took many days to create a new habit of positivity. I will start today, to be a more positive person, and I know it will have a positive impact on my health, my family, and my students. It's a choice that I have to make every day, and some days I struggle, but it's definitely worth it.

Multiple World Champion Team Roper, Walt Woodard, who I mentioned earlier, said that it takes thirty-one days to create a habit. This can be a destructive habit of negativity or a habit of building people and programs up. You decide. Walt's team roping partner for many years, Jake Milton, would say, "If someone asked me about another person, and I didn't really care for them, my response was always, They're okay."

I have to make up my mind that I like my horses and students. If a horse can feel the touch of a fly they can definitely feel an anxious heartbeat of a rider, and that puts them on the defense, and they will fight or flight. Our students are the same. They sense the negativity from their educators and they go on the defense and learning shuts down. They sense it in our body language and in the tone of our voice.

A Little History...General George Washington faced enormous negativity from many of his officers and thousands of his soldiers during the American Revolutionary War. They were desperately under paid, ill fed, and struggled with sickness and disease. Somehow, General Washington never lost focus of the ultimate mission. He never gave up hope, and he understood the power of positivity and being optimistic.

My wife and I are big baseball fans and one of our favorite players is former Texas Ranger Elvis Andrus. He, is a two time All Star Shortstop that is noted for his positive energy. It seems, Elvis is always teasing and joking around. It's rare to not see him with a smile on his face. Often, he is seen helping a younger player and celebrating when they make an awesome play. All Star slugger, Joey Gallo said, "The reason I love and respect Elvis a lot, is just, he's always himself. He brings that certain charisma, and that energy and positivity to the field every day." (Associated Press, Feb. 19, 2020). He is definitely a team leader that is very well respected by all players.

Educator funny:
Teacher: OK class, please settle down.
Teacher: Let's all calm down and get to work.
Teacher: Seriously guys, let's get quiet now.
Teacher: Everybody, let's bring the volume down.
Teacher: I SAID STOP TALKING AND GET TO WORK!
Student: Teacher, why are you so cranky today?

Chapter 4
Do Ground Work
(Share, Care, and Build Relationships...We are
Family)

It is my strong opinion that educators are strong and resilient, but we are perhaps the largest group of honest, caring, loving, nurturing, and fair people that want to do what is best for their students and co-workers. We wouldn't be in this business if the ALL MIGHTY DOLLAR was our main motivator.

Since we live and work around most of our students, we not only know them, but we usually know their parents, grandparents, siblings, aunts, uncles, etc. We see them at sporting events, stock shows, the grocery store, post office, at church, and work together in the concession stand on Friday nights.

We show up to support our students at One Act Play competitions, basketball games, and don't think for a moment they don't notice if you are there or not. We haul them around town, gathering cans of food for the yearly FCCLA food drive, and pick up garbage on the side of the highway with the NHS members community service project. We contribute to nearly every kind of fundraiser imaginable and when your spouse is a teacher as well, this can be an expense in the hundreds of dollars per year, way over the yearly $250 tax deduction.

On a more personal note, we visit our students when they are in the hospital or homebound. We attend their weddings, graduations, and other celebrations. I have also attended several of my students' funerals, which is incredibly heartbreaking. Educators cry when our students move or graduate, but are so joyful and thankful when they return to the school just to hug our neck, say hello, and share their accomplishments.

I've always believed the difference between a good educator and a great educator depended on how willing the educator was in developing a trusting caring relationship with their students. A good educator can be educated, know their content, have effective discipline strategies, and be successful on their standardized test, but a great educator loves their kids. I have heard Cheryl Whitefield, a respected, long time high school educator from Spearman, Texas say about challenging kids, "We can't wish them away and we can't wash them away, so we just have to love them." Mrs. Whitefield is a loved educator and a favorite among the kids at Spearman High School and has had a positive impact on thousands of lives over the years.

Cultivating a relationship with your students is not difficult. Every morning, we walk into the front door of the school building and see our kids. That first kid is our first opportunity to show we care and the opportunities are right in front of us throughout the entire day.

Take a personal interest in them, and be a good listener. Be sympathetic with their ideas and thoughts, and let them know you care. These actions will reap great dividends.

My first year, I taught 4th grade at Lampasas, Texas. My principal, Mr. Tim Petty, was a great educator. He really cared about the students and was ready to remind the teachers that our students were little people, but they had big feelings and emotions. They get sick, hungry, scared, etc. and these feelings are very real.

In 2002, I was teaching junior high in Hamilton, Texas, when a student aide came to my classroom to tell me I had an important call in the office. It was Shane Vonschriltz, a friend of my dad, and later a dear friend of my family. They had been outriding at Arlington Park Horse Racetrack in Chicago, Illinois. Dad had a massive, sudden heart attack and was on life support.

That afternoon I was on a plane headed to Chicago. I met my two sisters at the hospital and after talking with the doctor, we decided to let dad go. Needless to say, our lives were in a numb whirlwind for days. I had no prior experience with handling these types of things, even if I could think straight. The racetrack held a beautiful ceremony and paid to have dad's body flown back to Texas.

When I arrived back in Hamilton, the entire junior high staff was there. They had prepared food that fed everyone. They were on standby for anything we needed. They were amazing. I will never forget what those amazing educators did for me and my family. Over the next several years, we were there for each other many times. We built a family relationship that would become the most memorable years in my career.

Clinton Anderson, the famous horseman from Australia, is one of my favorites when I'm looking for techniques and tips while working with my horses. People bring him horses that buck, rear up, kick, bite, spoiled, and soured. Before he saddles one of these sweet darlings up, he may spend one to three weeks in the round pen doing groundwork. He will ask these horses to move and pivot, back up, and get soft in the body and mind. Then he is ready to saddle one up. In essence, he has built a relationship with that horse, getting them to do what he wants them to do because the horse finds comfort in the change.

If you have a pencil handy, you may want to underline these next two sentences.…**Building relationships may be the MOST important thing an educator can do with their students, fellow educators, parents, community members, and administrators. It takes time and effort, but the payoff is enormous!**

How do you build relationships? It's simple, spend time with that person and genuinely show you care about how they are doing and feeling. Work through challenges together and be a good listener. It's not about you, it's about them! I know you've heard this before, but I think we can become so over inundated with policy, requirements, regulation, and life that we sometimes forget. Focus on The Positive!

When I was a little guy, I would visit my granny during the summer. Her name was Anne Rountree, from Ballinger, Texas. She had taught forty-seven years, retired, then she substituted another ten. I thought my granny was the greatest person in the world, and it wasn't just because she spoiled me by baking fresh apple pies and making coke floats. I thought she was the greatest because so many people in that little town loved her. Someone always had something nice to say when we went to the post office or drug store. Former students would drop by her house just to say hello and sometimes share their woes of life. They felt comfortable knowing that she genuinely cared and loved them.

I can't tell you how many times I have been approached at teacher workshops in the central Texas region and asked, "Are you related to Anne Rountree?" after they read my name tag. I would say yes, and then the tears would start, followed by a story about how they loved Mrs. Rountree.

My granny lived in a small white house on the edge of town, drove a used car, and lived on a tight budget, but she was the richest person in the world. She had such a positive impact on so many lives. They may not remember what she taught them in English or History, but they knew she loved them.

"People will not always remember what you say, but they will always remember how you make them feel" Maya Angelou

Special Note: I would encourage every educator to keep all the special notes, cards, and letters from fellow educators, parents, and students. They are golden to me. I keep every one of them and read them often. They keep me going when the stress settles in.

Chapter 5
Smell of a Horse Melts Stress
(Rest)

Don't you just love the sound of that word? "Rest"

I mentioned earlier that for one year my job duties included being the principal at a Pre-K through 12th grade campus, teaching 4th and 5th grade math, part time counselor, bus driver, part time maintenance, worked the concession stand regularly, and anything else that may come up. That's part of working at a rural school, right? I survived, and I mean, I survived for one year. I'm not sure when and even if I slept. I truly believed that I wouldn't make it another year in education if I kept it up. I must also tell you that I'm the type of person that can't leave their work at work. I would take all the day's problems home and dwell on them entirely too much. I was a worrier. My mom always told me that I was born an old man. I worried all the time, even as a kid. With years and experience, I have done a pretty good job of kicking that bad habit, and that's what it is. It's a bad habit!

For the past eight years, I have taught dual-credit American History to juniors and dual-credit Government and Economics to seniors at Spearman High School. Both groups have a lot on their plate. These are the students that cry if they don't make A's. They are also the students that participate in several extra-curricular activities, and many have jobs after school. They burn the candle at both ends. Hmm, sounds like some educators that I know.

I love teaching the content, but feel like my biggest job is to help these students manage their time, learn how to take efficient and effective notes, stay positive, manage expectations, meet deadlines, etc., so they can be successful and not burn out and quit. I tell them it's like running a marathon, find what works for you, find your pace, and don't set your expectations so high that you will set yourself up for failure. We talk about going to bed at a decent hour and going to sleep. That means, turn their device OFF, and that also includes notifications! That thing that keeps their brains from resting. I've read several articles that say it takes the brain one to two hours after we turn our devices off for our brain to actually rest. We don't mind resting other parts of our body, but for some reason we don't think that our brain need rest as well.

Teacher funny: I can always tell which students stay on their device after they go to bed because they suffer from the thirty-pound head syndrome. They come into class and before the tardy bell rings, I hear a thud because their head has hit the desk, and they are sleeping.

Educators do the same. We go home after a hard day at school, check our social media or stream in our favorite program, and stay there until we fall asleep in the chair. My dad always said the invention of the recliner was humankind's biggest downfall.

I ask my seniors to write a note of encouragement to those juniors that I mentioned earlier, the ones with A LOT on their plates. I post the signs in my room, so I can refer to them over and over. One of my favorites was written by senior Fili Avila,

"Don't Worry About It, because if you do, you will put yourself through it twice."

Turning your brain off at night, so you can rest, can sometimes be a very difficult thing to do. I have found that I can rest better at night if I improve my diet and follow an exercise routine.

Teaching is usually not a profession that requires a lot of physical activity, so why are we so tired at the end of the day? The answer is simple...Stress.

I've always believed the younger the student, the more work and stress it puts on the educator. I teach high school, and I can tell you without a doubt, my wife that teaches fourth grade math, works twice as hard as I do. If you have some time, pull up the state requirements for fourth grade math, and you will be stunned and amazed. She usually gets to school by 7:00 A.M. and usually gets home around 5:00 P.M., and then she nearly always has papers to grade and lessons to prepare. No wonder she is always tired!

This example could probably fit for most teachers to some degree, so what can help? Jennifer loves her horse, Dollar. That is her hobby, and if she misses a day of riding or at least a day of grooming and feeding, she can tell the difference. She always says that just the smell of the horse makes stress go away. Maybe it's the smell we associate with enjoyment or relaxation of the horse, whatever, it works. Kind of like the smell of my mom's house. It's a smell of rest. We always kid around about some company making that horse smell in a cologne or perfume.

Hobbies of some sort make the mind escape and give it rest. I enjoy my horses, but I also enjoy writing. Whatever your hobby is, don't put it down. Keep going with it, if it provides rest and relaxation and if you don't have time, make time because at the end of the day, if you are spent and stressed to the max, everyone loses. You lose, your family loses, and your students lose.

Exercise! I know that may not seem like rest, but it does wonders for the mind, soul, and body. I started exercising regularly about seven years ago, and I wish I would have, thirty years ago. I can start or end my day with a regular exercise routine, eat healthy food, and rest well. I feel better about myself and love it when I go in for my yearly health checkup and the doctor says, "'I wish my blood pressure was as good as yours," and the doctor is twenty years younger. I can't express enough how much regular exercise and eating healthy can melt away stress, and give you a better quality of life. If you don't already have an exercise program, get one!

Educator funny: You can always tell a teacher at a restaurant because they are always the first to finish their meal. We get about 20 minutes to eat lunch, really 15 or less, if we don't have to help the kids get settled in the cafeteria. Then it's like watching hogs going to the slop trough, food begins to fly!

Chapter 6
Read Your Horse
(What We Can Change)

What characteristics make a good teacher, and what makes a great teacher?" I've spent many hours driving my pickup down the highway, or riding my horse, pondering this question. I think a good teacher loves their students and knows and enjoys their subject content, but I also think a great teacher reaches out to students developing relationships to teach.

Teaching and educating is about learning, and learning should be the main objective that we strive for in this calling.

Having said that, I realize that can be a seemingly impossible task at times for many reasons. I hesitate saying that, but it's very true. We cannot change home situations, we can't do brain surgery, and we can't control challenging genetics, but sometimes, we think we can. That's hogwash! Do you really think you are that good?

I've taught hundreds of kids over the years, of all ages, that qualified for special services. I've set in countless Parent, ARD, and 504 meetings, where new goals were set then I've left wondering, "How in the world am I supposed to do that?"

One student in all of the years stands out. This young man, a fourth grader, was a sharp kid. We spent many hours that year talking about his horses, dogs, and life in our rural setting. There was little doubt his intelligence was high, but he struggled reading. My heart really went out to him because you could see the frustration, pain, and heartache this guy felt when asked to read, and I was his reading teacher. I counseled with the special education teacher, the principal, his parents, my mentor, and anyone else that I thought could give me some insight to help this little guy. In the end, he was diagnosed with Receptive Phonological Awareness Disorder.

He was immediately given extra help from the Dyslexia teacher, and I began learning about his challenge, so I could accommodate in the classroom. We met with his parents, and by the way, they were as or more relieved as everyone else, to know why their son hated to read so much. If you are a parent, you know how much it hurts when your child hurts. The one statement that I'll never forget that helped me so much came from the dyslexia teacher. She said, "We can always strive to learn about Dyslexia, and we can always help the students cope with this learning difference, but we cannot fix the problem." I felt like a ton of bricks fell from my shoulders. I would continue to learn about Dyslexia and help many others learn to cope with it, but I know, I cannot make it go away, and I cannot "fix" it.

That year I started writing my first Gunpowder book, Gunpowder, *Tales of a Wise-Cracking Cowpony* with this young man in mind. The number of words on a page, the size of font, and number of illustrations was and still is a huge factor in writing the series. I will never forget the time a parent came to me in tears, telling me that her daughter with Asperger's read Gunpowder. She was fourteen years old, and it was the first chapter book she had ever completed.

Van Hargis, a world renowned horse trainer, says "Horsemanship is to always study your horse. Learn their strengths and weaknesses on the ground and in the saddle. We can study every day in every aspect. Learning to read your horse better prepares us as horsemen and women and can ensure not only our safety, but he horse's as well. Do you know your horse's strengths and weaknesses?"

I believe a great teacher does the same with their students. It's work that is continuously in progress. Sometimes there is success, and sometimes there isn't, but we must always continue to read our students and know our limitations.

Important Note* I am personally not a big fan of state mandated curriculum, standardized tests, and government policy, but I understand why we have them, and I also understand that I have to comply, so I do, and try not to gripe about it too much. **I would encourage you to do the same and go on and educate, work your magic, build relationships, love others, and make a real difference in the lives of so many.**

If you feel a strong desire to make changes in these areas, please follow correct protocol, and uphold the integrity that makes us professional educators. I have served on committees at the regional and local levels, testified in front of the Texas House Education Committee in support of a bill, and have been instrumental in writing the scope and sequence for Social Studies curriculum at the state level. Lawmakers want and need our input, so I would encourage you to get involved and follow proper procedure if you feel led to make policy change. Be a part of the solution, not part of the problem.

Teacher Funny….If you really want to appreciate what and who you teach, go spend ten minutes in an early childhood room. The energy level could power any major city for a week! I really admire those teachers!

Chapter 7
Getting bucked off
(It's Okay to Make Mistakes)

Do you recall the Happy Days episode when Fonzy had to admit when he was wrong? He tried so hard to say it, but he couldn't spit it out. He tried and tried, and then he finally got it out, all womperjawed. I have personally felt the same way. I am educated, experienced, and a self-proclaimed expert in a little bit of a lot of little things, so why is it so important to admit that I am wrong from time to time? Well, here's why.

It shows our student's that we aren't perfect, and that we are human. Caution: Before you do this, make sure to ask your students to refrain from ridiculing you. I make this announcement on the first day of school when many of the students are still shy, scared, and subdued. My student responses are usually smiles of empathy, confusion about why I'm not perfect, or little ornery grins, and wheels grinding on how they can catch us. I don't think they understand how difficult it can be to talk, listen, think, and write at the same time, but they sure get a thrill when they catch me in a mistake. I do believe most appreciate it, and know they can relax when they make a mistake.

Turn mistakes into learning opportunities. I sometimes make the mistake on purpose to see who can correct me. Some things to consider: What was the mistake? Why did I make the mistake? If I made a mistake, it will probably be easy for my students to make the same one.

I sometimes get the impression that students and their families believe teachers live at school and are surprised when they see us at the grocery store or around town. How many educators live in the back room of the school house and have to haul coal or wood to heat up the stove located in the center of the classroom? Can't say I've ever had to do that.

Most baseball fans love a home-run hitter. Every team usually has at least one player that can really launch a ball into the stands. The average strikeouts per home run is about six and a half. This means the home-run hitter will strike out six to seven times before he hits the big one. I wonder if these hitters get down on themselves from time to time? I'm sure they do, but they continue to not dwell on the mistakes and swing for the stands the next time up to the plate.

Being an educator is kind of like riding broncs in a rodeo; it's not if you are gonna break a bone, it's when. (Chances are you won't break a bone teaching) It's not if you will make mistakes, it's when. We learn and grow from our mistakes. I know because I have made them all, and I survived, and most importantly, my student's survived. Occasionally, I'll get a thank you card or a nice comment in an email from a former student thanking me for this or that, and usually, my first thought is, "Thank God, I didn't mess them up!"

Teacher Funny...We were learning about colonization of North America in 10th grade World History...I asked, "What was the name of the ship that carried the Puritan's to North America in 1620?" One student confidently sounded out "The Cauliflower!"

Chapter 8
Don't Ride the Trail Alone
(Make Friends, Be a Role Model/Mentor)

Veteran educators, this one is mainly for you. We have dropped the ball, and it has already come back and hit us in the nose-hard. We have lost so many educators from so many of the negative aspects of public education, and I believe if we did a better job mentoring these young people, they may stay in the profession where they are badly needed. Let's analyze the situation,

Young Buddy and Gloria (these names belong to our dogs) just graduated from a university, where they have just spent the last four or five years preparing for their lifelong dream of being an educator. They want to make a positive difference in this crazy world in which we live, but after the first week, Buddy and Gloria begin to question and panic over what they have done. They have realized the expectations are overwhelming, the students are very difficult to manage, and they are treated like they have the bubonic plague by many of their peers. They give it the ole college try, but more than half drop out before year five is up and go into another profession.

We can't let this happen!!!

So what can we do? For starters, ask to be their mentor. You don't have to be appointed by an administrator, or you may, either way, ask to help. I have had several awesome mentors throughout the years. Paula Petty, from Hanna Springs Middle School in Lampasas, Texas, was my first mentor, and she would spend hours with me every week creating lessons for our fourth graders of which many qualified for special education. She gave me such a strong foundation that would benefit me for many years to come. As time went on, I would teach at four other rural Texas school districts where I would find an educator that I admired. I would watch, learn, and listen to them as much as possible. Now it's my turn to give back.

Over the years, I have mentored many teachers new to the profession in an official capacity and unofficial. After the first time of being a mentor, I realized that I was the one blessed. I made a great friend, and from that friend, I would grow. These young professionals or even older professionals that are entering the education field for the first time, are loaded with valuable ideas, skills, and information. We need to recognize and honor those talents.

Ideas in being a good mentor and friend:

- ✓ Be a great listener...just hold your tongue, even though we've been there, done that.
- ✓ Before correcting, give honest praise about something right.
- ✓ Before you criticize, try to think how you were as a new educator. Did you make the same mistakes, or worse?

- ✓ Don't say or do anything that diminishes a person in their own eyes.
- ✓ Propose or plant questions and ideas.
- ✓ Make the fault easy to correct. You might say, that's a common mistake, or I can see why you would want to do that.
- ✓ Most importantly….Be a great role model and that includes not being a whiner and a gripper with a negative attitude. All educators need to be lifted up, but if you cast a negative influence on a newbie, they are sure to fail.

My good friend, and state and national award winning educator, Mrs. Kristi Ramon is our Teacher Quality and Mentoring Coordinator at Spearman I.S.D. She spends a great amount of time helping new educators in the district deal with managing the classroom environment, understanding the learning process, working in the community, and just about anything a new professional educator needs. She has also been an incredible listener, motivator, mentor, and friend to many older educators like myself. I can't imagine Spearman I.S.D. without Mrs. Kristi Ramon.

Teacher funny… One year I had a 7th grader ask if he could go to the restroom, I said yes and he went. He came back soaking wet from head to toe. I asked what happened and he said, "The urinals were overflowing and I slipped and fell!"

Chapter 9
Become a World Champion
(Develop Your Craft)

Fred Whitfield, an eight-time World Champion calf roper grew up in a very poor African American home in East Texas. He was fortunate enough to live across the street from a family that had horses, calves, and an arena. The family saw a talent in Fred and sort of adopted him and supported him throughout his entire career. The one thing that set him apart from some of the top ropers in the world was his determination to get better. He roped 50-90 calves a day, six days a week. He developed a craft that put him among the best PRCA cowboys of all time. I believe his self-drive, focus, and motivation to be the best, made him a World Champion, not his eight gold buckles. He sharpened His Craft every day.

When I was just a young lad, my mom, Caroline Landry, took my sisters and I to 4-H horsemanship clinics, horse shows, and play days. She and my dad made sure we had good horses, but mom made sure we would become knowledgeable and skilled horsemen and women. She made sure we weren't afraid to try new things and encouraged us to have a strong work ethic, critical tools needed to develop and sharpen a craft.

Teaching Social Studies is my craft. I've taught 4th grade through 12th grade Social Studies, AP World and U.S. History, and dual-credit U.S. History, Government, and Economics. When I'm not teaching, I'm usually reading historical nonfiction and fiction. I listen to history podcasts and Audibles when driving my bus route. In the summer, I attend Social Studies workshops, conferences, and lectures. I look at Social Studies topics from a cultural, social, historical, political, and economic perspective. Spearman, Texas High School is the center of my universe, and I am passionate and serious about what I do, and I love getting better at my craft. I feel good about what I do, and I know that I'm pretty good at it, and that's a wonderful feeling to have.

We preach to our students to always learn, challenge yourself, stay updated in their future professions, and we need to do the same. It's so easy for life to get in the way. Raising our kids, being a supportive wife or husband, being involved in church and community soaks up our time, money, and energy and it doesn't leave much time for self-growth, but we need to practice what we preach. If we don't grow as educators, our students won't grow, and we fall behind. We can fall in a rut, we count the days until the next holiday or retirement, and become miserable. I know, I've been there.

So, how do I start to get out of the rut? Easy, start with a problem and establish a goal or vision. Last year, I had a class that I just couldn't reach. I reached way down in my bag of tricks, but nothing seemed to work. My fellow Social Studies teacher and friend, Todd Nies, told me about Choice Board. He had success with it, and thought I should give it a try. This style of teaching put more control and responsibility with the student which meant I had to let go and I admit, this made me feel very uncomfortable. I knew I had to try something new because what I had been successful with in the past, was not working.

Todd and I spent many hours discussing and planning our lessons, and he was a tremendous help. I started using Choice Board with my sophomore World History students, and it worked. Todd and I gave a presentation on Choice Board through our local service center, and it has been a tremendous blessing getting through the many 2020 challenges. This old bird learned something new, and I am a better educator for it.

If you want something you've never had, you have to try something you've never done.

Our world is changing fast, and the way our students learn is changing with it. Put a device in the student's hands, and they become engaged. I have learned to teach virtually this year. I'm learning the importance of learning by implementing YouTube video and podcast in the lessons. Today, employers are not looking for experts in Social Studies, Science, English, and Math. They are looking for employees that can communicate effectively, problem solve, and think creatively. Let's be a role model for our students, and I promise our students will notice, and maybe they will look at us the way Fred Whitfield's fans did. Maybe, just maybe, our students will view their educators as a World Champion.

We have so many valuable teaching tools that we didn't have ten years ago, but we have to take the initiative to accept the challenge and try. Warning! We may fail, like so many challenges we try the first time. How many times have you told your students that it's okay to fail? Just pick yourself up, make changes, and try again. Same goes for us. Personal and professional growth takes patience, perseverance, and strength, but we as educators are no stranger to any of these.

Educator funny...You know you work in a rural school when "Dead Skunk in the Middle of the Road" is played on the intercom between classes.

Chapter 10
Stay in the Middle of Your Saddle
(Getting a Handle on Classroom Management)

Setting the course on the first day of school - Hello students (with a smile), my name is (your name), and I am happy to be your teacher! I want you to know that I believe that God has put us together for a very special purpose.

I want you to know that I care about you, and that I take being your teacher very seriously, and I promise to give you all that I have this year. We have many things to learn, and they all will require self-discipline and the understanding up front that you will struggle, but I will meet you halfway.

If your behavior is not acceptable, I will talk to you about it and make sure you know what the expectations and consequences are. I promise to use common sense, be flexible when necessary, and be as fair as possible before I administer the consequences. I want you to also know that I will be structured, consistent, and be certain that I follow through and I do what I say. (This is critical!)

Most of all, I want you to remember we will learn new exciting things this year. We will have fun, and I truly hope we get to know each other soon.

Okay Cowboy or Cowgirl, take a deep seat and get a faraway look in your eye because the rodeo is about to start!

I can't completely say that I've been there and done that because I am still learning. Remember, every year we have a new set of young individuals that come to our classes. They are all different. There is not another person in this entire world that is just like Sally or Jim. That means they are unique with unique gifts, talents, emotions, and needs. They may be about the same size and age, but they are truly young individuals. You can't program them to get the desired outcome, and that is why building relationships with them is the utmost importance and it may need to happen every day.

Yes, they need structure and they need discipline, but they also need love and understanding. They want empathy, just like we do as adults.

I follow several equine clinicians that talk about "problem horses" and how to correct them. These horses may kick, bite, rear up, flip over, run away with the rider, etc., and the "fix" is always the same from every equine expert, build a relationship, until they are soft in the body and mind and are ready to learn.

I will take this horse to the classroom, which is a round pen, about sixty feet in circumference. Just the horse and me, I want his complete attention. I ask the horse to do something that I want him/her to do, and when the horse responds positively, I praise the horse. When the horse responds negatively, I make it uncomfortable for him or her to behave that way. If the horse is barn sour, always wanting to run back to the barn, I work him or her at the barn. Before I ever step up in the saddle, I make sure softness in the mind and body are established, then a relationship has been created or redeveloped. It is very critical that I don't get back on until this happens.

I have become proactive in establishing a strong positive atmosphere between me and this "problem horse" and it's the same within my class if I follow the same idea. We have class rules that usually say or imply "if you do this, this will happen." If we count on this reactive mindset, you will not have the positive, learning environment that you should be looking for. I teach high school kids, and I will tell you this reactive mindset won't work! They will continue to kick, bite, and rear up on you! It's the same for many junior high, middle schoolers, and elementary kids. Rules need to be posted in the classroom, but the way they are worded can help create the culture and atmosphere for the classroom.

I have a colt that will be two years old this Spring, which means he will be ready for his first riding. I've been doing a lot of ground work in the round pen which includes leading, backing up, asking for softness in the neck, pole, and body. I also ask him to move his hind quarters and shoulders. He loads and unloads from the trailer pretty well, so he should be easy going for the first ride, right? The first ride will definitely be in the round pen and my wife will be by my side while being on her horse to ease the colt's worries, but I need to be ready for anything when I step up in the saddle.

The colt may jump sideways from a leaf blowing, jump or buck from the weight or pressure on his back, and it will probably be this way for the first thirty rides or so. It is critical that I stay in the Middle of my Saddle. This means that my body is perpendicular to the horse. I'm not leaning over or leaning back. My butt is planted in the seat of my saddle. It's important that I have a very keen sense of awareness at all times to what is going on around me as well as the colt's body language, and it is very important that I do not clamp down, give off a sense of insecurity, or tension, because the colt will pick up on it and take advantage quickly.

If I know my students and know what to look for, I can stop a problem from happening or react in a way that minimizes the problem.

Five ways to help you stay in the Middle of Your Saddle:
- ✓ Set your students up for success
- ✓ Build relationships and gain respect
- ✓ Be consistent and thorough
- ✓ Have a keen sense of awareness at all times
- ✓ Know how and when to react. Allow students to make a mistake before we correct them.

I am proud to say that I have sent only one student to the office for disciplinary issues in the past seven years.

Teacher funny...One day I asked a student if he enjoyed lunch in the cafeteria. He rolled his eyes and looked up and said, "It beats starvation!"

Special note from the author:

I mentioned in the Purpose of this Book that I would talk more about the TREA award, and why I needed a "win" so much. Prior to winning the 2019 Texas Rural Education Association Ruth Long Teacher of the Year Award, I was counting the days to retirement. Worse, I wasn't sure if I could make it. I felt that I had done about everything I possibly could to feel satisfied and fulfilled as an educator, but there was a big hole, and I was miserable.

The application for the TREA award made me dig way back and think about the previous twenty-plus years in education and it occurred to me that I really had made a difference.

Winning that award and being at the convention was one of the greatest weekends of my life. I met so many school board members, administrators, and fellow educators that genuinely cared about kids. They treated me like a superstar! **They treated me like I had value and that was my "win" that changed my teaching career.** On our way home from the convention, I realized that I had lost focus on the most important part of being an educator, making a difference in the lives of my students and this was my fault. I got lost in curriculum, standardized scores, and checking the years off.

Now, I still love teaching at Spearman High School. My administrators and fellow educators are amazing. We have a fantastic school and we work hard to be successful in so many ways, and I love being a part of our winning team. I told my wife Jennifer that I needed to give something back to my profession. That is what this book is about. I pray that every educator that uses this book will gain some insight that will help them Rein in Educator Stress because our profession is definitely worthy.

If you feel that this book can benefit you, place it somewhere handy, so you can refer to it when the stress settles in.

2 Timothy 1:7 KJ version...For God hath not given us the spirit of fear: but of power, and of love, and of a sound mind.

About the author:

My name is Michael Rountree, and I am an Educator. Since 1995, I've worked in five rural districts, which include Lampasas, Hamilton, Walnut Springs, Cranfills Gap, and now Spearman, Texas. I graduated from Tarleton State University in Stephenville, Texas with a Bachelor of Business Administration in 1992, a Texas Teaching Certificate from Region 12 Alternative Certification Program in 1995, and a Master of Education from Tarleton with an emphasis in Educational Administration in 2005.

I'm certified in grades 1 through 6 self-contained, special-education, social studies composite, educational administration, and a CDL bus driver's license. Since 1995, I've taught all subjects in fourth and fifth grade, elementary and junior high special-education, fourth through 12th grade Social Studies including AP and dual-credit, principal for a Pre K through 12th grade school, and drive a school bus. I currently teach Honors World History, Dual-Credit U.S. History, and Dual-Credit Government and Economics at Spearman, Texas High School.

My honors, accomplishments, and awards include being the guest speaker for the 2006 graduating class at Walnut Springs, Texas High School and the 2010 graduating class at Hamilton, Texas High School, 1998-1999 Reading Renaissance Master Teacher, 2001-2002 Teacher of the Year for Hamilton I.S.D., and I was also awarded the Texas Rural Education Association Teacher of the Year in 2019. I am the author of the award winning Gunpowder children's book series which includes *Gunpowder, Tales of a Wise-Cracking Cowpony, Gunpowder the Cowpony Goes to Cowboy School, and Gunpowder, Rivals on the Ranch.* www.gunpowderandconrad.com

I grew up on the back of a horse in the hill country around Brady, Texas, which is where many of the stories and ideas come from for my Gunpowder books. I spent many hours watching and listening to my father talk about training horses, and I have implemented many of the same techniques in my teaching.

Today, my wife Jennifer, a fourth grade math teacher, and I, together, have five children and three grandchildren. We love living in the country with our horses, dogs, and chickens just outside of our hometown, Spearman, Texas.

If you have a question or comment, send me an email at **rountree123@gmail.com** and I'll try to respond as soon as possible.

I want to give a very special thank you to the following people for their selfless encouragement and insight that helped in the collection of experiences, thoughts, and ideas for this book:
My amazing wife and teacher Jennifer Rountree, mom, Caroline Landry, student Filiberto Avila, and friend, Shane Vonschriltz. Also, friends and very experienced fellow educators Kristi Ramon, Kelly Carrell, Cheryl Whitefield, Dan Raibourn, Tim and Paula Petty, Todd and Terri Nies, Dixie Smith, Wendell Neff, Katherine George, the late Randy Edwards, Clay Montgomery, Celia Rountree, and the Texas Rural Educators Association.

I also want to thank Amanda Nies, a very talented teacher and digital illustrator, for her exceptional work in designing the cover.

Notes